HEALTH AND SOCIAL CARE

Preparing to work
in
adult social care

LEVEL 1

Rebecca Platts

D1374874

E160098

Nelson Thornes

Contents

Introduction

Reed Social Care and Community Care

Reed Social Care is the UK's leading recruitment consultancy for high-quality, dedicated social care staff. From a nationwide network of offices, we find work for qualified and unqualified social workers, community support and residential work professionals, throughout the public and private sectors. For those people who come to work for Reed, we offer industry-leading training and support, to enable people to progress their careers.

Reed Community Care provides support and carers directly to those in the community. We run extensive training courses, and offer support throughout, in order to provide the best possible care to the people we work with.

Entering the adult social care job market

The social care job market is a challenging one to enter at the present time, particularly in the public sector where budget cuts mean that organisations are seeking to employ only the highest-quality staff that they can find. Managers are looking for professional, conscientious employees who really want to work in the social care sector, and who display commitment and enthusiasm for supporting the people that they care for on a daily basis.

However, an ageing population also means increased demand for high-quality care staff – something that will continue for the foreseeable future as a greater proportion of the population requires support and care. With the right help and application, you really could find yourself in a job for life.

The purpose of this book is to help you to complete your Level 1 Preparing to Work in Adult Social Care qualification and to gain your award. It also aims to help give you the tools to get a job in the adult social care sector, through work based examples and Reed employment hints and tips.

Expert help

As the leading recruitment consultancy for social care staff in the UK, Reed Social Care is ideally placed to advise new workers on entering the sector, from building a CV, to finding work experience and interviewing for the ideal job for you. We help hundreds of people each week to find work, in both temporary and permanent positions, and we want to share our experience with you.

That's why, throughout this book, you will find helpful hints from our highly experienced consultants, all designed to help you find that perfect job in adult social care. These tips range from advice on CV writing to interview tips and techniques, all linked in with the learning material in the book.

As well as this, Reed Social Care has gained insights from some of our biggest clients – leading recruiters within the adult social care sector – to help you understand the mindset of a potential employer. This includes the traits and skills that they would like to see in their new employees, why you need the skills taught in this book, and how they are used on a day-to-day basis within their organisations.

This is invaluable information and offers a unique insight all geared towards helping you to gain a position within adult social care.

reed.co.uk

Throughout the book, there will also be regular mention of reed.co.uk.

reed.co.uk is the UK's number 1 jobsite, featuring jobs advertised by many different employers, as well as posts advertised by Reed's consultants on behalf of their clients.

All of the positions advertised on the site are listed by sector, and are easily searchable by location, salary and type of position, to make finding a position which is right for you as easy as possible.

reed.co.uk allows you to register as an individual user and to create and download your CV online, using advice from the experts along the way. There will be regular advice throughout this book to help you to improve your CV and covering letter, and how to use them to apply for the positions which are right for you.

reed.co.uk is an ideal starting point for those looking to find a job within adult social care, and provides all the tools to enable you to improve your career prospects while learning with this book.

About this book

Welcome to your Preparing to Work in Adult Social Care Level 1 Course Book. The purpose of this book is to help you complete your Level 1 Preparing to Work in Adult Social Care Award. This book gives complete coverage of the qualification and includes expert employment advice from Reed Social Care to help you get a job.

This colourful text is packed full of activities to check what you have learnt and there are also exclusive tips from Reed Social Care.

The book's features include:

Unit opener – this page contains a brief introduction to each unit along with the learning outcomes you need to achieve.

'Think about', which encourage you to think about issues in health and social care.

'Find out!', which encourage you to do further research.

'Did you know?', with key supporting information, such as legislation you should be aware of.

Reed Social Care @work give insights from employers into which skills they value in their staff.

Key Terms

'Key terms' – during your course you'll come across new words that you may not have heard before. These words are in bold in the text and the definitions have been provided.

In Practice
What would you do?

'In Practice' and 'What would you do?' – a range of real life examples of different scenarios to provide context to the topics covered. Some of them ask how you would approach the problem.

Reed Social Care tips are designed to help you get a job.

Your questions answered

'Your questions answered' – your expert authors answer some burning questions you may have as you work through the units.

'Quick Quiz' – at the end of each unit you will find ten multiple choice questions which recap what you should have learnt in the unit. Check your answers to the Quick Quiz questions with your tutor. Answers can also be found in the 'Care' section of www.planetvocational.co.uk.

Good luck!

Introduction to the adult social care sector

This unit aims to introduce you to adult social care (ASC) in its various forms. You will find out how people with different support and care needs may achieve an extended quality of life within a variety of settings. You will also look at the role of informal care.

On completion of this unit you will:

- know about types of social care support available to adults
- know the range of jobs available in adult social care.

1.1 Know the types of social care support available to adults

There is a wide range of adult social care in England. When you work in social care the people you support may use several types of support, services and resources. You need to be aware of these so that you can support people appropriately.

What is adult social care?

Adult social care (ASC) is the support and services used by people who need support to keep themselves healthy and safe, and to live as independently as possible. Its aim is to help people achieve the **quality of life** they choose.

People may need practical support to complete personal and daily living tasks. These include:

- washing and dressing
- preparing and eating meals
- housekeeping and shopping
- paperwork and personal finances
- laundry.

find out!

There are several verbs (doing words) used in the Learning Outcomes and Assessment Criteria for this qualification that you need to understand. These are 'Know', 'Define', 'Outline', 'Identify', 'List' and 'Give examples of'. Go to www.planetvocational.co.uk/subjects/care/preparing-to-work/572-preparing-to-work-in-adult-social-care-level-1 to find out what they all mean.

Quality of life A good quality of life is having a good standard of health and well-being, with opportunities to access education, work and leisure.

Key Term

People sometimes need emotional as well as practical support. They may find it difficult to express how they are feeling. We will look at communication skills in Unit 4.

As a care worker it is very important that you work in **partnership** with the people you support. We will look at partnership working in Unit 5.

The Health and Social Care Bill (2007) says that adult social care should **enable** and **empower** individuals within a safe and supportive environment so that they can live the lives they choose.

This includes not only receiving support from care-based services, but also enabling people to access **community facilities**, education, work and social networks.

think about

There are community facilities that may be available to people in your local area, for example:

- leisure centre
- church
- supermarket.

Think of a few more and how they benefit local people.

Key Terms

Partnership Working together with another person or an organisation.

Enable Support someone by providing them with the means, knowledge and opportunity to continue to do as much as possible for themselves for as long as they can.

Empower Enable someone to take control and make decisions about their life.

Community facilities Places within a community provided by local or national government for the local community's benefit. For example, schools, hospitals and community centres.

Adult social care aims to provide a safe and supportive environment for **vulnerable adults**.

Your questions answered

What does providing 'a safe and supportive environment' mean?

This does not mean keeping vulnerable people in secure buildings. It means providing a safe and welcoming place where individuals:

- have the maximum choice and control over their own lives

- are able to carry out **supported decision making** about their lives

- are helped to consider and deal with the risks they may face.

Key Terms

Vulnerable adult A person over the age of 18 'who is or may be in need of community care services by reason of mental or other disability, age or illness; and who is or may be unable to take care of him or herself, or unable to protect him or herself against significant harm or exploitation'.
(from the 1997 Consultation Paper 'Who decides?', issued by the Lord Chancellor's Department).

Supported decision making Some people need support when making decisions. For example, deciding what to wear, what to eat, where to live or how to spend their money. When working with an individual you will need to find out how they express themselves when they make decisions, and help them to consider all the options.

The people you support will come from different backgrounds. You must always be respectful of their beliefs and preferences. You must treat everyone you support fairly, equally and without **discrimination**.

All social care support should meet the needs and rights of individuals. See Unit 2 for more information

Discrimination
This is when people are treated differently, unfairly or unequally because of their disability, age, gender, race or sexuality.

Key Term

think about...

What rights does someone with a disability have? Answer: The same as you!

Types of social care support

The main types of social care support are listed below.

Day services
Day services provide support for older people, adults with physical or learning disabilities, and adults with mental health needs. They can be drop-in centres, or centres where people can meet others who may have similar support needs. The supported adults take part in activities such as art or gardening.

Day services are referred to as 'day opportunities' or 'community support' when they take place in smaller community venues rather than in large buildings.

Day services can provide people with the support to try activities like music and photography

There are also specialist day services, for example for people who have a brain injury or high support needs due to a medical condition. Staff in these settings are often registered practitioners. These qualified professionals must register with a professional body in order to work. For example, a mental health nurse must be registered with the Nursing and Midwifery Council (NMC).

Residential support including respite care

This type of support includes group homes for a small number of people, or large residential homes with many bedrooms. Care homes provide accommodation and personal care. Some are registered for nursing care, and registered nurses cover and carry out certain aspects of care, such as administering medicines. Community nurses provide health care in residential homes not registered for nursing care.

In Practice

Support at Brook Dean

Thomas, Maggie and Anna live in a bungalow in Brook Dean. They have a contract with a support agency called 'My Life' and employ a staff team of 12 people. The team includes care assistants and support workers who provide Thomas, Maggie and Anna with support to live at home within their own community.

Domiciliary support

Domiciliary care workers visit people in their own homes and support them with daily living tasks, such as washing and dressing. The workers may be agency staff or paid care workers.

Community support

Currently, much of the support available is provided within a person's own community: in smaller meeting places or in a person's own home.

Support purchased using personal budgets

This is when a person uses their **personal budget** to employ personal assistants to support them with everyday tasks.

Respite A short period of time when an individual or their carer can have a break. For example, the supported individual could go to a centre providing specialist care, or a care worker could stay with them in their own home.

Personal budget An amount of money provided by the local authority and given directly to an individual so they can arrange their own support. The individual is able to spend it in a way that makes sense to them and meets their assessed needs.

Key Terms

find out !

- What other types of support and services are used in your local area? For example, laundry services, meals on wheels, sitting services.

- How person-centred are they? Can they be arranged to suit an individual?

- Research different types of service and support – look on the internet; gather leaflets from your local GP's surgery, Citizen's Advice Bureau and council offices.

In Practice

Maz and Julia

Maz: 'I was born with a physical disability which has meant that I have needed support all my life. I am an active campaigner for Disability Rights and train social care workers for the local council. I employ three personal assistants to support me every day.

Julia is my personal assistant. She supports me with some personal care, such as washing my hair and cutting my nails. I use an electric wheelchair and Julia makes sure that this is always fully charged. Three days a week, Julia supports me at work. She helps me to carry equipment and paperwork, as well as manage my appointments diary.'

Maz – an Employer and Social Care trainer – with Julia, her personal assistant

In Practice

Ray

Ray lives by himself in his own home. He was recently widowed. His daughter and her family live about three hours away by car, but they try to visit Ray at least twice a month.

Ray had an assessment for care from his local county council. This showed that he needed support in the mornings to get washed and dressed, at mealtimes and to prepare for bed. He also needs support with his housekeeping, shopping and laundry.

Penny is Ray's neighbour. She shops for him and generally keeps an eye on him.

What support and services do you think could make a positive difference to Ray's life?

Ray – recent changes in his life mean that he now needs some support

> **Review** When an individual and their support circle consider the support they have been receiving and whether or not it meets their support needs.

Key Term

Users of service groups

It is important to remember that some individuals will be included in more than one service group – for example, an older person who also has a physical disability.

Service group	People who need support
Older people	People over the age of 65
Individuals with disabilities	People with physical disabilities which may mean that their mobility is restricted or they need support to manage daily living tasks
Complex needs	People who may need support with medical conditions or have high-level care needs requiring 24-hour support People with mental health problems or learning disabilities may also have complex needs
Individuals with learning disabilities	People who may have difficulty communicating or making decisions and require guidance and support with daily living tasks
Individuals with mental health needs	People who have a mental health condition
Individuals with dementia	People who have dementia

Users of service groups

Tip

Think about any informal care that you may have provided in your life, to friends and family, or volunteering in the community. Make a note of anything you think of – this can be useful information when creating a CV for prospective employers.

What is the role of informal care?

Informal care means care and support that is carried out by people who are not paid to provide it. For example, a family member or friend providing care at home, or a neighbour giving a lift to their church or mosque.

Many people with support needs live in their own homes with informal family support to carry out daily living tasks, such as washing, dressing and preparing meals.

It is important that informal carers are also offered support. Plans should be agreed and in place in case the carer is no longer able to continue their support.

Many other people receive informal support with their laundry and shopping. They have neighbours, family or friends who regularly 'check in' on them.

Informal carers are an important source of information for professionals as they know the individual and their support needs very well. When a care manager wants to **review** the support an individual receives, they work in partnership with the individual and their carers. The manager will meet them to talk about what is working well and what needs to change so that the person and their carers are better supported in the future.

think about…

What informal support do you receive on a daily basis?
List five examples of informal care and support that you receive. For example:

- other parents collecting your child from school
- a colleague giving you a lift to work
- a neighbour feeding your cat when you are on holiday
- your partner cooking you a meal.

find out!

Use the internet to research local organisations that provide support for informal carers. What kind of support do the organisations offer?

- Carers UK: www.carersuk.org
- Carers Direct: www.nhs.uk/carersdirect
- The Carers Trust: www.carers.org

Penny

Penny lives next door to Ray, whose wife Pamela died recently. Penny helps Ray by asking him if he needs any groceries when she goes shopping, and sometimes she cooks Ray a meal and takes it round to him. When her husband mows their lawn, he also mows Ray's for him. Penny is good friends with Ray's daughter, Jane, and often phones her if she is at all concerned about Ray.

Penny provides informal care to her elderly neighbour

1.2 Know the range of jobs available in adult social care

What jobs will be available to me?

There is a wide range of jobs within adult social care (see pages 14 and 15). A career in social care is very rewarding; it is satisfying to know that you have helped make a positive difference to someone's life.

In Practice

Gavin – care worker

'I recently cared for my elderly uncle who had lots of health problems. He is now living in Extra Care Housing with support. I chatted to his carer one day and she said that her agency was looking for staff, so I applied and got the job! I now support people with lots of different support needs, helping them to get washed and dressed, prepare meals or do the vacuuming and dusting. I get to know some of the people I support really well.'

Jobs offering direct support

Job role	Setting	Key tasks
Residential care and support worker	Works in residential homes supporting the people who live there Works shift patterns that include waking nights and sleeping in shifts	Personal care Meal preparation Cleaning Administering medication Maintaining relationships with families and friends
Day care officer	Works in a day service, Monday to Friday	Completing person-centred reviews Accessing the community Supporting personal care needs
Domiciliary care worker	Works with people in the community	Personal care Shopping and preparing meals Accessing community facilities Developing and maintaining social networks Supporting individuals to take medication
Personal assistant	Employed directly by an individual to support them with their everyday life Paid out of the supported individual's personal budget	Personal care Shopping and preparing meals Cleaning and laundry Supporting with paperwork and finances

The range of jobs offering direct support

Jobs offering indirect support

Role	Key tasks
Managers	Planning and organising the service and support Responsibilities for staff, including recruitment, supervision and training Responsibility for the health and safety of people and buildings Administrative duties, including answering the telephone, using a computer and filing
Housekeeping staff	Cleaning and laundry
Trainers	Providing support and training to staff

The range of jobs offering indirect support

Jobs requiring medical-based training and qualifications

Role	Key tasks
Psychiatric or mental health nurse	Provides specialist nursing care to people in health care settings, such as surgeries or hospitals, mental health units and day services, or out in the community
Registered nurse	Provides medical specialist care, advice and support to individuals living in their own homes or in residential and nursing homes
Occupational therapist (OT)	Works with individuals to find out what activities will help them to remain healthy and well Provides advice about equipment that will increase a person's mobility and independence, such as wheelchairs, bath and shower equipment as well as equipment to support eating and drinking
Physiotherapist	Uses physiotherapy to increase a person's mobility which may be restricted due to illness or disability Aims to improve someone's quality of life by limiting pain and increasing independence
Clinical psychologist	Diagnoses mental illness and works with the person to understand, prevent and relieve the symptoms
Psychiatrist	Specialises in the diagnosis and treatment of mental disorders Authorised to prescribe psychiatric medication

The range of jobs requiring medical training and qualifications

Tip

REED
SOCIAL CARE

Think about the range of jobs available (you could look in reed.co.uk to see examples of jobs in your area), and begin to research which of these would best suit your skills. If you are able to do voluntary work in these areas, this will dramatically increase your chances of securing a position later on.

think about

Regardless of what level or type of job you work in, always ensure the people you support are fully involved in any planning or decision making about things that directly affect them and their support.

In what settings is adult social care delivered?

We have previously looked at the types of support available. Let's now look at where that support may be provided.

Setting	Care delivered
Residential and housing settings	Homes for older adults including **sheltered housing**, **extra care** and warden-controlled housing Care homes – with and without nursing Rented property where people have a tenancy agreement with a private landlord, support organisation or housing association Group settings for adults with learning disabilities Specialist residential homes, for example for people with dementia
Community-based settings	Day services, **community hubs** and community groups held in, for example, a mosque or a village hall Day care for older adults Life skills training centres or colleges for younger adults with learning disabilities Any setting based in the community, such as a café, pub or leisure centre

Settings in which adult social care is provided

A young man being supported to ice-skate. Always think 'out of the box' when it comes to community-based settings!

Key Terms

Sheltered housing This is a group of independent and self-contained flats or bungalows. Some will have a manager or warden living on site or nearby to provide support.

Extra care This is similar to sheltered housing. Domiciliary care workers are on site and there are set times for visits. Additionally there are staff to help with emergencies. Support is available 24 hours a day.

Community hub A centre managed by three or more community groups which work to improve the quality of life for the whole community. It is similar to a drop-in centre.

What qualifications do I need? What career pathways are there?

Opportunities to gain qualifications include:

- apprenticeships, which are nationally recognised schemes combining work with learning and training

- competency-based qualifications which demonstrate that you are able to perform the skill, trade or occupation

- knowledge-based qualifications to help you gain the understanding and knowledge you need to carry out your role

- higher qualifications, which depend on the route you wish to follow and include management qualifications.

There are various career pathways available to you within the different sectors. For example, if you wanted a career in residential care, you could begin as a support assistant and work your way up to becoming a support worker, then senior support worker, then assistant manager and then manager.

Tip

It's always worth thinking about what route you might take to get to your desired position. It may be that you need to gain further qualifications along the way – some employers will sponsor you for these.

find out!

Look on the internet or in your local newspaper and find examples of social care jobs advertised in your area.

A local authority

We have a range of jobs available within social care, so we look for a real variety of people to work with us. If the first job you try doesn't suit you, don't give up on social care as a whole – often there is something different you can try which you might enjoy far more. Gaining qualifications and shadowing senior workers is a good way to open doors to new positions.

@work

Quick Quiz

1 What is social care?
   a. Practical support and care for a range of people in need of care and assistance
   b. Support with household chores only
   c. Support and care to just attend social occasions
   d. Support and care just for people with disabilities

2 What is 'informal care'?
   a. Support from a care agency
   b. Care and support from someone who is not paid a wage
   c. Support from a community health visitor
   d. Care from a registered nurse

3 What is 'respite'?
   a. An assessment for equipment
   b. A break for the carer or supported person
   c. A community funding programme
   d. A technique for pain management

4 Which of the following is NOT a community facility?
   a. Mosque
   b. Leisure centre
   c. Private swimming pool
   d. Village hall

5 Which of the following is NOT a type of social care support?
   a. Day centre
   b. Community hub
   c. Visit to the cinema with a community support worker
   d. An ambulance service to an out-patient appointment at a hospital

6 Which activity would a personal assistant NOT support someone with?
   a. Planning their support
   b. Performing medical procedures such as injections
   c. Cooking a meal
   d. Opening and responding to post

7 Which of the following is NOT a job in adult social care?
   a. Support worker
   b. Residential care worker
   c. College support assistant
   d. Medical supplies salesperson

8 What is NOT an apprenticeship?
   a. An opportunity to study for a qualification while working
   b. An opportunity to earn a small wage whilst learning
   c. An opportunity to study at college to gain a qualification before starting work
   d. An opportunity to observe and shadow people in the area you want to work in

9 Which of the following is NOT a quality required to work in adult social care?
   a. Unreliability
   b. Flexibility
   c. Sensitivity
   d. The ability to maintain confidentiality

10 Which of the following activities would you NOT support someone to undertake if you were a support worker?
   a. Brushing their teeth
   b. Rock climbing
   c. Organising a taxi to town
   d. An illegal activity, for example theft

Introduction to the
values and principles
of
adult social care

This unit will give you an understanding of the key principles and values that are an essential part of adult social care in a multicultural society.

You will find out why it is important that you uphold these key principles at all times, and understand their benefits to both staff and individuals.

You will also learn about the importance of using personal histories, together with knowledge of the likes, dislikes, needs and wishes of individuals, to support choice and quality of experience for the people that you will support.

On completion of this unit you will:

- know the values and principles of adult social care
- know the importance of diversity within adult social care.

2.1 Know the values and principles of adult social care

It's important to be punctual for work, and wear smart clothes.

A value is a standard of behaviour that we believe to be important. Our values influence everything we do. For example, Jayne believes it is important to arrive at work on time and to be dressed appropriately.

A principle is a guiding rule or belief for personal behaviour. It is often based on culture and religion. Principles shape what we believe to be right or wrong. For example, Mike believes it is wrong to tell lies.

We live in a **multicultural** society. In social care you will work with and support a range of people. As individuals they will have different personal **beliefs** and values.

I try to be honest and truthful in all areas of my life.

Multicultural
   Including people of different races, languages and religions.

Belief A principle that an individual holds and believes to be true.

Key Terms

What are the key values and principles in adult social care?

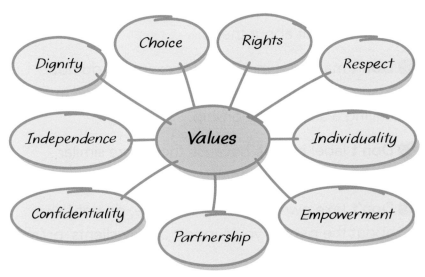

The key principles of care

think about

What are your values? Personal values include being honest, trustworthy, committed, friendly and loyal.

- Write down five values that influence the way you behave.

- How do you demonstrate these values? For example, do you show that you are passionate about the environment by only buying items wrapped in packaging that can be recycled?

- Now think about how you treat other people who hold different values from yourself. Would you treat someone less favourably if they threw all their packaging into the general waste bin?

Tip REED SOCIAL CARE

It is always worth researching the organisation that you want to work or volunteer for. Understanding their values and principles is central to demonstrating that you could become an useful member of their team.

Individuality

It is important to respect people's individuality. To be able to support each person as an individual, you will need to find out about them.

🌑 **Don't** make assumptions. For example, do not assume that older people are not interested in having a sexual relationship.

🌑 **Don't** label people because they share similar support needs to others.

🌑 **Don't** take ownership. For example, do not talk about the people you support as 'my clients' or 'my patients'.

Everyone has a unique identity

Person-centred
When someone is involved in any discussion or decision about their life, with their needs and wishes placed at the centre of that discussion.

Key Term

The people you support should have a **person-centred** care or support plan which shows what is important to them and how they want to be supported.

Choice

An essential part of your role as an adult social care worker will be to ensure that people are given choices and have a role in making decisions about how they live their lives.

In Practice

Supported decision making at Brook Dean

Thomas wants to re-decorate his room at Number 3, Brook Dean.

Thomas and his key worker, Josh, spend time looking at Thomas' person-centred plan to find out what Thomas likes and dislikes. Thomas says in his plan that spending time alone in his room is important to him. The plan shows that Thomas is a huge music fan and likes the rock band, Queen. Josh asks Thomas if he would like his room to be a place where he can spend time relaxing and listening to his music. Thomas agrees.

Thomas does not use spoken words to communicate, preferring to use a mixture of symbol cards and pictures, so he and Josh look through music magazines seeking inspiration. Thomas has a large framed poster of Queen. He decides to decorate his room in the same style as the poster, using black, silver and chrome.

How did Josh ensure that Thomas was in control of how his room would be decorated?

Answer: Josh used different ways to support Thomas to make choices about how his room should be decorated. He used pictures in magazines and referred to Thomas' person-centred plan.

Dignity and respect for the individual

When people treat us with respect and dignity we feel valued and important.

Always treat the people you support with respect and dignity. You can do this by:

- making sure people have choice and control over the support that they receive

- supporting them to express their views and opinions

- using clear communication so that you are easily understood

- supporting people to have good standards of personal hygiene

- making sure that people have privacy, by respecting their personal space and personal information

- not ignoring them

- celebrating their achievements

- showing that you understand how people feel when different life events and situations happen to them.

find out!

You can find more information about the principle of 'dignity' by entering 'Dignity in Care' in the search box on the website: www.scie.org.uk

In Practice

Anna

Anna really enjoys going out to cafés and restaurants to meet friends, eat new and different foods, and to 'people watch'.

Due to her disability, Anna needs support to eat; she finds it difficult to swallow and can sometimes choke and cough on her food. She gets embarrassed when this happens in public. She likes to be supported to eat discreetly, with her wheelchair positioned so that her back is to other customers.

It's important to Anna that her support worker makes sure Anna has lots of wipes and aprons packed when they leave Brook Dean to go out. This is so that, as soon as she has finished eating and has cleaned any spills, she can position her chair to face the rest of the room – to people watch.

Independence

You will need to think about what support each person needs to be as independent as possible. Seemingly small things can make a big difference; for example, having a key to your front door or carrying your own mobile phone.

Partnership

Often, several support people are involved in one person's life. See Unit 5 for more information about partnership working.

Support people to be as independent as possible

The following rights are defined in the Human Rights Act (1998):
- the right to life
- the right to liberty and security
- freedom of thought, belief and religion
- the right to marry and start a family
- protection from discrimination
- the right to education.

Rights

The people you support have the same rights as you and other people in the UK. These rights are protected by law. They keep us all safe from harm and give us the freedom to control our own lives and to take part equally in public life. See page 47 and Unit 5 for information about duty of care.

Privacy and confidentiality

The people you support will often have to share their homes with other residents, staff and visitors.

You must always support people to protect their privacy. Remember to:

- close doors when supporting people with personal care

- knock before entering bedrooms.

You must work within the laws governing how information is kept. These laws include:
- The Data Protection Act (1998)
- The Human Rights Act (1998)
- The Freedom of Information Act (2000)
- The Disability Discrimination Act (2005)

The Data Protection Act (1998) states that records should:
- be kept in a safe place
- be kept to a minimum necessary to achieve their purpose
- only be used for the purpose they were collected
- only be available to those who need to see them.

You must also support people to protect their private information. Always put paperwork away, and store it securely and correctly. When you no longer need paper files, destroy them securely by shredding them. Always use secure passwords to protect any information that is kept on a computer. Shut down computers when you have finished working on them.

Always check with the person you support that they agree to their information being shared. Check with a senior member of staff if you are unsure about whether or not information should be shared.

People have the right to access their personal records and read everything that has been written about them.

Empowerment

Above all it is important that you support people to become empowered. This means making sure that the supported person's voice is heard in any decision making, and that you support them to challenge any **inequality** in their life.

think about ...!

How important is privacy to you?

- Where do you go when you need some time alone?

- Do you lock the door when you use the bathroom?

- How do you protect your private information, such as your bank personal identity numbers (PINs) or medical records?

Inequality Unfair differences (not equal) where one group or individual has less of something than another group or individual. For example, inequality in employment may mean there are more jobs available for able-bodied people than for those with a disability.

Key Term

Why do you need to uphold these values and principles?

Positive experiences and well-being

If you provide positive experiences and person-centred support, the values and principles that we have explored in this unit will naturally be achieved.

Legal and organisational requirements

The law sets out rules about how organisations should provide adult social care and what the **outcomes** should be for the people they support. Organisations have policies and procedures in place to make sure these rules are followed.

Many social care organisations have a mission statement. This sets out how they work to uphold the values and principles of adult social care in the support they provide.

Outcome The result achieved from an action.

Key Term

find out!

Find an example of the mission statement of a social care organisation and see if you can identify the values and principles we have discussed so far in this unit.

Anti-discriminatory practice and human rights

Values and principles must be upheld to promote anti-discriminatory practice. People must not be treated differently, unfairly or unequally because of their disability, age, gender, race or sexuality.

In Practice

Maz

Maz is about to set off to meet some friends at a restaurant in town. Julia, her personal assistant, rings ahead to check that there is disabled parking available near the restaurant. She is told that the restaurant does not have disabled parking spaces, and that the restaurant is not designed for people with disabilities.

The restaurant is discriminating against Maz because of her disability.

People with disabilities have a right of access

We all have rights, and the people you support have the same rights as you. You should support people to ensure that they are able to enjoy the freedoms that these rights bring. Support people to challenge discrimination by providing them with information to communicate their wishes and make complaints.

Rights versus responsibilities

Sometimes we may find that our responsibilities as a worker can be at odds with the rights of the people we are supporting.

The supported person's right to:	The adult social care worker's responsibility to:
Have their own front door key	Safeguard the individual from harm
Confidentiality	Report and investigate anything that may cause serious harm or exploitation to the individual Share private information with new colleagues who will be supporting the individual
Be free from physical restraint	Use wheelchair straps to ensure a person does not fall from their wheelchair
Go out in their community	Ensure that enough support workers are available to safely support everyone and meet their needs

Rights versus responsibilities

Confidentiality versus 'the right to know'

As you will work closely with people in social care, you may be told confidential information. Occasionally you will have to make a decision between respecting confidentiality and deciding that the information needs to be passed on to someone with 'the right to know'. Talk to a senior member of staff if you are unsure about whether information should be shared.

What would you do?

Josh recently supported Thomas to meet up with his friend Dave at the pub.

As Josh brings drinks to the table he overhears Dave telling Thomas that his support worker keeps borrowing his CDs and not returning them. Josh asks Dave if he has told anyone where he lives about this. Dave hasn't because he is afraid that his support worker will be angry with him. He asks Josh not to say anything.

🔵 What should you do if you were Josh?

Answer: Josh needs to consider if Dave is at serious risk of harm or financial exploitation. He should talk to Dave about the effects of what is happening. Josh should talk to his manager for advice if he is unsure. He should explain to Dave that he may have to tell his manager, and why.

What if your own values and principles conflict with those of adult social care?

How similar are your own values and principles to those that we have discussed so far in this unit?

You might sometimes find that your own views are different from other people's. It is important that we recognise that we all hold certain **prejudices** in life. You will need to find a way to respect and support other people's values and choices even when they conflict with your own.

Prejudices
Opinions that are made without knowing or considering all the information. For example, we may judge someone based purely on how they look without knowing anything else about the person.

Key Term

Your questions answered

My religion says that I must not eat pork. What should I do if I am asked to prepare bacon sandwiches and eat these with the people I support at Brook Dean?

Answer: It is important that your beliefs do not affect the experiences of the people you support. However, you should certainly not have to eat the bacon. If you are uncomfortable about preparing the bacon, then let your colleagues know and ask them to support you by taking on the task for you.

Management of resources

There can often be a conflict between meeting a person's choice and the management of resources, such as money and staffing. For example, if there are not enough staff on shift, then the choices for the people being supported will be restricted. Or, if there is not enough funding for a service, it will have to reduce the amount of support it can offer to people.

Organisational policy

Organisational policies can conflict with the rights of individuals. For example, the Manual Handling Policy of an organisation may state that two people must support someone with lifting from seated to standing for health and safety reasons. This could mean that someone has to remain in their seat for longer than they wish to, until two support workers are available to help.

Balancing the needs of the family and the needs of the individual

Balancing the needs of the family and the needs of the individual you support can sometimes be a challenge.

Good support always takes into account the views of an individual's family even if they are different from those of the individual. However, the family's views should not override those of the individual.

Remember: Your key responsibility is to make sure the individual you are supporting is in control of their own life, and at the centre of all decisions made about their support. Sometimes you may need to support the person to challenge their family's views.

Where issues and conflict cannot be resolved, you should seek support from your manager.

A leading charitable organisation

We will always look for staff who share our values and principles as an organisation, and I will always check at interview whether the applicant has really done their research about us and actively wants to work for us, or if this is just another job to them. It is important that our staff share a desire to promote our values and principles, so that we are all pulling in the same direction towards a common goal.

think about

Have you ever had to persuade your parents or caregiver to let you do something? (For example, to go on holiday alone with your friends for the first time.)

- Was it a challenge?
- Did your views conflict with theirs?
- What were their concerns?
- Was it easy for you to understand and accept their concerns?
- How was the situation resolved?

2.2 Know the importance of diversity within adult social care

What makes you different from other people?

- How old are you and what is your gender?
- Do you have a physical disability?
- What is your sexual orientation?
- Do you practise a religion or faith?
- What is your background and where were you born?
- What are your beliefs?

Do you experience discrimination in your life based on your answers to the above questions? How do you challenge this discrimination?

Why is it important to support and respect diversity within adult social care?

Everyone is different – not just different physically because of appearance but also different because of age, gender, ethnicity, faith and beliefs, culture, abilities, sexual orientation and social class. This is called 'diversity'.

Promotion of individual rights

As a social care worker it is your responsibility to support people's individuality. You should respect the differences between individuals and challenge people who do not.

Tip

Social care organisations work with a variety of individuals from diverse backgrounds. If you have experience which could be beneficial (such as speaking a second language), make sure this information is on your CV. This can set you apart from other candidates.

Empowerment and recognition of individuals

If you do not respect and support diversity, this could lead to unfair and unequal treatment. It may have a harmful effect on someone. You can respect people's diversity by working to empower them and promote their individual rights.

Supporting choice

You can support people to make decisions and have control over their lives by giving them information. This should be in a format appropriate to their level of communication.

Reducing the risk of discriminatory practice

When people experience discrimination, the effect on them can be harmful. To protect people, there are laws in place to promote everyone's right to fair and equal treatment, regardless of their differences.

It is important that people with different support needs are seen accessing ordinary facilities and taking part in their community. When you work in adult social care you will have an essential role to play in promoting diversity.

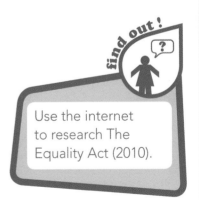

did you know?

In England and Wales, the General Social Care Council (GSCC), which regulates social care work, states: 'As a social care worker, you must protect the rights and promote the interests of individuals and their carers.' This includes 'Promoting equal opportunities for individuals and carers' (1.5) and 'Respecting diversity and different cultures and values' (1.6).
www.gscc.org.uk

Why is it important to find out about an individual's history, needs, wishes, likes and dislikes?

Use a person's personal profile or **personal history** to help you to support them in a way that is suited to their needs and values (see next page).

Reference to someone's personal profile or history will:

find out!

Use the internet to research The Equality Act (2010).

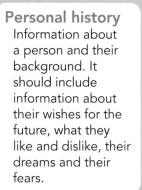

Personal history
Information about a person and their background. It should include information about their wishes for the future, what they like and dislike, their dreams and their fears.

Key Term

Holistic approach
Considering a person's whole life, not just parts of it.

Key Term

Each person you support will have a different background, needs, hopes and dreams

help to enrich the quality of support they receive

enable a holistic approach to their support

make it possible to prevent negative experiences by finding out what they dislike or are fearful of

help them to make personal choices.

did you know?

Further information and guidance about values and diversity can be found on the following websites:
- Care Quality Commission, www.cqc.org.uk
- Direct Gov, www.direct.gov.uk
- Social Care Institute for Excellence, www.scie.org.uk
- Skills for Care, www.skillsforcare.org.uk
- Skills for Health, www.skillsforhealth.org.uk

Quick Quiz

1 Which of the following is NOT a value of adult social care?

  a. Respect   **c.** Rights

  b. Confidentiality   **d.** Discrimination

2 Which of the following is NOT a Human Right?

  a. Protection from equality

  b. The right to get married

  c. The right to vote in free elections

  d. Protection from discrimination

3 Which of the following is NOT an example of respecting someone's dignity?

  a. Leaving someone in soiled clothes until you are ready to support them

  b. Supporting someone to maintain their personal hygiene and appearance

  c. Providing someone with equipment to help them to eat

  d. Locking the bathroom door

4 There are eight essential elements of person-centred support. Which of these is NOT one?

  a. Making sure support staff are able to make decisions without involving the individual

  b. Ensuring medical charts are recorded accurately

  c. Ensuring the individual has choice and control

  d. Listening to the individual and their needs and wishes

5 What does 'GSCC' stand for?

  a. General Standards of Care Commission

  b. General Social Care Council

  c. General Skills Council Corporation

  d. General School of Care Compliance

6 Discrimination is when a person is treated:

  a. like everyone else   **c.** unequally

  b. rudely   **d.** humanely.

7 If you were a social care worker and were told something in confidence, in what situation should you break this confidence and tell someone else?

  a. If the person is at risk of putting a friendship in jeopardy

  b. If you suspect the person is lying

  c. If the person is at risk of serious harm

  d. If the person is at risk of being made fun of

8 How could you ensure that a family's needs were taken into consideration when planning social care support with an individual?

  a. You shouldn't even consider this as it must only be about the individual's needs, not the family's

  b. You should listen to them and take account of their views and then disregard them

  c. You should email them explaining why they are making the planning process difficult and suggest they don't attend the next planning session

  d. You should listen to the family's views, and respect their values. If necessary, you should then support the family and the individual to consider risks and action plans to manage these.

9 Which of the following is NOT a value?

  a. Respect

  b. Pain

  c. Loyalty

  d. Trustworthiness

10 Which of the following in NOT an example of diversity?

  a. Our culture

  b. Being human

  c. Our religion and beliefs

  d. Our sexual orientation

Awareness of the
skills and attitudes
needed to work in
adult social care

Working in adult social care requires more than the ability to deliver physical support. In this unit you will find out about the wide range of skills required to enable individuals to achieve the quality of life that they choose.

You will also find out about the attitudes required, and reflect on your own attitudes and skills, identifying those areas which would benefit from development.

The aim of this unit is to develop your awareness of the skills and attitudes needed to work in adult social care.

On completion of this unit you will:

● know the range of skills and attitudes essential to work in adult social care.

3.1 Know the range of skills and attitudes essential to work in adult social care

Adult social care provides care and support for individuals to achieve the quality of life they choose.

The people you support will have different support needs: physical, emotional, intellectual and social. To meet these support needs you will need to have a range of **skills** and attitudes.

Skill The ability to do something and to do it well.

Key Term

What are your needs?

- Physical needs, such as the need to eat, sleep, keep warm and be safe.
- Emotional needs, such as the need to be liked, to love and to be loved.
- Intellectual needs, such as the need for mental stimulus, learning and communication.
- Social needs, such as the need to belong, be accepted and have relationships.

Tip

REED SOCIAL CARE

Job descriptions for positions often only display the tasks that will be required to complete a position. You can impress your prospective employer by considering the additional skills and attitudes that might be useful.

Essential skills

Communication skills

The key communication skills are: writing, reading, speaking and listening. You will need good questioning techniques, and the ability to understand information in a variety of formats, both written and spoken English.

These skills will be used to gather, record, interpret, share and report information. For example, you will need to record information in communication books and personal files, and report changes. You may need to write emails and other electronic reports, but many records will need to be handwritten. Take time to write clearly so that others can read and understand what you have written.

Tuesday 19th February
On shift: Karen, John and Fran
When I started my shift Anna was still asleep. She woke up about 8.15 am and was supported to have a shower. I supported Anna to wash her hair and then to brush her teeth. Anna's gums were bleeding. I have made an appointment for Anna to see the hygienist on Friday (22nd). Anna chose a blue tracksuit to wear. Anna had two weetabix for breakfast, but left half of this. Then Anna was supported to the bus for college with a packed lunch. She took the ingredients required for her cooking class. She is due to be collected at 3pm.
Fran Jacobs

Social care workers often need to write in communication books, so that they can share information with colleagues to ensure that people receive seamless support

think about

How will you support people:

- to manage real life events, such as births and deaths?
- to build and maintain their relationships and friendships?
- to set and achieve goals to improve, gain and maintain their independence?
- to access other services, such as housing, education and health?

think about

Can you think of any situations you have been in where you have misunderstood a note or message from someone?

Always speak slowly and clearly so that others can understand. For people who do not use verbal communication, use their preferred way of communicating, such as pictures and symbols.

did you know?

Royal Mail hired 'address detectives' to work out addresses written on letters and parcels in handwriting that was impossible to read. Can you imagine the cost of this? Countless medical mistakes are made due to unreadable notes.

Some people use pictures and symbols to communicate

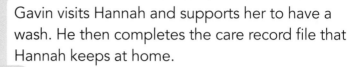

In Practice

Gavin

Gavin visits Hannah and supports her to have a wash. He then completes the care record file that Hannah keeps at home.

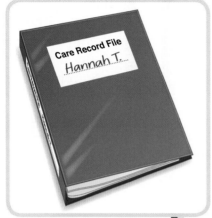

Gavin writes down the time he arrives, how he supports Hannah, and any issues or messages he needs to communicate to the morning agency support worker. Today, he writes a note to tell them Hannah has very sore skin on her hip and that he has supported Hannah to apply some medicated cream to the area.

What communication skills does Gavin put into practice when visiting Hannah?

Answer: Gavin writes in the personal file how he has supported Hannah and leaves a written message for the morning support worker.

Listening skills are essential for a social care worker. Listening to people properly and effectively takes time and practice.

When you are working with an individual who may communicate in different ways, remember:

- to be patient – they may need time to respond

- to avoid ending the person's sentences – instead guide and prompt them, using questions

- to listen with your eyes! Observe their body language and expressions.

Information and communications technology (ICT) skills

You use ICT skills daily – for example, when you use a mobile phone, computer or photocopier.

If you are not confident about your ICT skills, ask your manager for support and training. You could also access free online tutorials or attend adult education classes.

ICT skills will also enable you to support people to use interactive games consoles, television and music technology.

- Many people now use video calling software. It is of particular use to those who are unable to travel or leave their homes due to their support needs.
- Individuals can order shopping online and use social networks to contact friends and family.
- Many people work from home online.

Maths skills

Social care workers need to be able to add, subtract, multiply and divide numbers, and to check calculations for accuracy. Maths skills are needed for a range of activities, from recording the amount of fluids an individual drinks to recording information on petty cash records and supporting individuals with personal money records.

Tip REED SOCIAL CARE

On your CV, remember to include useful skills which may not be specific to social care. ICT skills are a good example as they are something which all employers look for.

find out!

Various branches of technology help improve people's mobility, independence, and ability to communicate with others.

Use the internet to research different types of 'assistive technology'.

Recording and interpreting skills

In this unit we have considered the range of records that you will have to complete, particularly:

● communication books

● individual personal files and communication diaries

● care records.

It is vital that you take time to interpret the information gathered from these records as they can show patterns of change in a person's behaviour or health. You need to be able to understand the information and use it to help you decide what action is required.

What would you do?

Josh has been off sick. When he comes back he starts his shift by reading the staff communication book and individuals' communication diaries. There are several pieces of important information:

Maggie's mother has sadly passed away, and Maggie has been very quiet. Workers have observed that Maggie has not been eating very much.

Anna has had some test results from the surgery which confirm she has a wheat intolerance.

No issues have been recorded for Thomas.

● What does this information tell Josh about how to support Maggie, Anna and Thomas?

Answer: Maggie's quiet state and reluctance to eat could be signs that she is grieving. Josh needs to be mindful of this when supporting Maggie. He should support Anna to not eat anything containing wheat. He should check with Thomas to see how he is.

Essential attitudes

An attitude is formed by how you think, what you do, and what you feel. When working in adult social care you will need to:

- be reliable and dependable. People rely on your support and could be at risk of harm or isolation if you let them down and don't do what is expected of you.

- be non-discriminatory. Being non-judgemental and valuing people's diversity leads to a better quality of experience (see Unit 2). You should not **stereotype** individuals.

- be responsible and accountable. You should be aware of your responsibilities, and of your **duty of care** to work within the organisation's policies and procedures, such as health and safety. You are accountable for your own actions.

- be able to cope with change. You should be open and respond well to change, especially if it improves the quality of life for the people you support.

- act responsibly within the setting. This means you must be mindful at all times of your professional responsibilities and be accountable for your own actions.

- demonstrate initiative. This means making decisions on your own and taking responsibility for them.

Stereotype To have a fixed idea about a type of person.

Duty of care Health and social care organisations have a duty of care towards the people they support. They must ensure that people are safe from harm.

Key Terms

Choose three essential attitudes. Write down how you show that you have this attitude in your own life. For example: dependability – 'I volunteer at a local charity shop, every Saturday from 8am until 1pm. I am always on time and have never missed a shift.'

Change can be unsettling. You will need to think about how you support people to cope with changes to their lives, and to their support.

How can you develop these skills and attitudes?

You will be responsible for continually checking and improving the quality of your work. You will need to **reflect** on what you do well and where your skills and knowledge need to be improved, and ways to do this.

Reflect Think about.

Key Term

Training courses are a good way to learn and develop skills

There are many ways to learn and to develop your skills and attitudes:
- attending courses
- obtaining qualifications
- using e-learning programs
- reading study guides and testing your knowledge
- watching DVDs or television programmes about working in social care
- researching on the internet
- reading trade magazines, for example *Community Care*.

Why is it important to continue to gain skills and knowledge at work?

- You need to keep up to date with legislation and policy changes, and understand how these will affect the way you work.

- You need to practise and refresh skills that you don't use regularly.

- Learning and training gives us opportunities to share good practice with other workers.

What could be the consequences of not keeping your skills and knowledge up to date?

- You could put yourself, the people you support and other workers at risk.

- You will not be able to progress in your career.

Think of a mistake you have made. How would you do things differently next time?

It is important that you learn from any mistakes you make. Reflect on the cause of the mistake, the consequences (what happened) because of the mistake, and what you could do differently in the future to prevent it happening again.

You will have regular supervision meetings with your line manager. This is an opportunity to discuss how things are going for you and to raise any issues you need support with. You can also use this time to consider what further information and training you need to improve your skills.

A UK care home group

Our staff need a variety of skills to successfully do their jobs, and having a well-rounded skill set is a real plus point. Apart from the obvious knowledge and training in care and the social care sector, we look for employees with strong communication and IT skills, and good written and mathematical skills. All of these will help you in a career in the social care sector, and hopefully assist you in progressing towards management positions later on.

Quick Quiz

1 Which of the following is NOT an essential skill for working in adult social care?

   a. Listening techniques

   b. Problem solving

   c. Speaking fluently in a second language

   d. Teamworking

2 Ned takes £20.00 out of his bank account; he spends £3.10 on a return bus journey into town and £4.22 on a chicken burger and chips for his lunch. He then spends £9.99 on a Kiss CD for his Dad's birthday. When he gets home he gives you the change and the receipts. You need to record this in his personal monies file. How much money does Ned have left?

   a. £4.99   **c.** £3.54

   b. £2.69   **d.** £2.19

3 Why is clear, accurate recording of information important? Choose THREE.

   a. It prevents mistakes from happening

   b. It keeps everyone informed and up to date

   c. It shows how neat your handwriting is

   d. It can be interpreted to see what changes need to be made

4 What type of attitude would it NOT be helpful to have when working in adult social care?

   a. Dependable

   b. Judgemental

   c. Enthusiastic

   d. Empathetic

5 Which of the following is NOT a type of support need?

   a. Physical   **c.** Social

   b. Touch   **d.** Emotional

6 Archie hurt his back when he went go-karting at the weekend. His doctor has prescribed him with strong painkillers. He must take these regularly: two painkillers four times a day at regular intervals, with food. There are four blister packs in the box; each blister pack contains 18 tablets.

How many tablets are there in total?

   a. 84   **c.** 44

   b. 96   **d.** 72

7 Within adult social care, which of the following is NOT a constructive practice for solving problems?

   a. Thinking of solutions

   b. Blaming people

   c. Action planning

   d. Reflecting on good practice

8 As a social care worker, why is it important to keep up to date with your skills and knowledge? Choose THREE.

   a. To keep up to date with current legislation and policy

   b. To win quizzes

   c. To provide quality support to individuals

   d. To develop and improve the support you provide

9 Which of these examples of ICT would you NOT use when working within adult social care?

   a. Computer

   b. Fax machine

   c. Mobile phone

   d. Social networking site

10 As a social care worker, why is it important to reflect on the support you provide? Choose THREE.

   a. To learn from your mistakes

   b. To find out if your colleagues like you

   c. To improve and develop your skills

   d. To identify how you can do things differently in the future

Awareness of
communication
in
adult social care

The aim of this unit is to develop your awareness of communication in adult social care.

You will look at the essential skills needed, how you can develop them, and how to overcome barriers to communication.

You will also learn about the range of records used when working in adult social care and how to complete them correctly.

On completion of this unit you will:

- know the communication skills needed in adult social care
- know how adult social care workers can meet the communication and language needs of individuals
- know the importance of record keeping in adult social care settings.

4.1 Know the communication skills needed in adult social care

Tip

REED
SOCIAL CARE
•••

Think about how you will communicate with prospective employers or recruitment agencies. First impressions are very important!

Communication is about giving and receiving information. The people you support will use a variety of ways to communicate, and they will need you to understand these so that you can support them to enjoy a good quality of life.

Skills

How can you encourage and motivate people to communicate?

You must respect the people you support and their right to have their views heard. Some people may find it difficult to communicate verbally, perhaps because of a disability, or because English is an additional language. Others may need you to use signs and pictures. You need to actively support people to communicate so that you can understand what they need and want.

Find out how a person prefers to communicate by asking them and spending time with them. Look at the **communication passport** in their personal file.

Communication passport This records how an individual chooses to communicate. They may use words, gestures, pictures, or behaviour.

For example:

When I do this: pat my stomach.

It means: I am hungry.

I would like you to: support me to eat.

Key Term

Actively support communication

Using verbal skills

You should speak clearly and slowly so that people understand what you are saying and can take in all the information.

When we talk, the pitch and tone of our voice changes to reflect how we are feeling. For example, when a person is happy and excited, they tend to speak quickly and with a higher tone of voice. When a person is feeling down, they tend to speak slowly and with a lower tone of voice.

Our **body language** and facial expressions tend to reflect what someone is saying – this shows that we are listening and that we understand.

Formal and informal communication skills

Use formal language (for example, 'Hello' and 'How are you today?') in the workplace, to write records and emails, and to answer the telephone. Make sure you use meaningful language and words that

Body language The position and movements of someone's body when they are talking or otherwise communicating. People are generally unaware of their body language and it often reveals how they are really feeling.

Key Term

people will understand when communicating with colleagues, other professionals and the people you support. This shows your professionalism and ensures that information is clear and easily understood by everyone.

We tend to use informal language with our friends and families (for example, 'Hi ya' and 'You good?'). It also includes **slang** (for example, the word 'dude' for 'man'). When you are at work, try not to use informal language. Try also to avoid **jargon**, and be very careful when using **abbreviations**.

Slang The use of informal words, such as 'grub' instead of 'food'.

Jargon Words used in a particular profession that may not mean anything to someone outside of that profession. For example, 'multidisciplinary team', which means 'a number of different people from different professions working together'.

Abbreviation A shortened word, such as 'meds' for medication. Abbreviations are common in social care and can cause confusion if everyone is not clear about their meaning.

Key Terms

Sometimes we may communicate informally with people that we know well at work. This is acceptable as long as we are always respectful and remember people's communication preferences. For example, don't shorten someone's name without their permission.

If people don't understand what you are saying, they may lose confidence in your ability to understand their support needs. This could lead to you supporting people incorrectly and putting them at risk of harm.

Listening is an essential tool at interview, or when registering with an agency. Displaying the ability to listen in interview is equally as important as speaking yourself. It will demonstrate to a prospective employer that not only will you be able to listen to individuals, but also to management on a day-to-day basis – this is key to self-improvement at work.

Using listening skills

You need to listen actively because it is important that the people you support feel they are being listened to. It shows that you value them and are interested in what they say.

Active listening is:

- Observing – give people eye contact and attention whilst you are listening.

- Repeating – say things back to people to show you have understood.

  For example, they say, 'I don't like blue, it doesn't suit me.' You say, 'You don't like blue because you don't think it suits you?'

- Summarising – provide the person with a summary of what they have told you.

  They say, 'I have tried to ring her loads of times but she doesn't answer the phone, she's got problems with her hearing. I do need to get hold of her, so I think I should send her an email.' You say, 'OK, you can't reach her by phone, so you will email her.'

- Reflecting feelings – show that you understand how the speaker is feeling.

  They say, 'I can't stand it when they talk to me like that and treat me like a five-year-old.' You say, 'That must make you feel very cross.'

- Interpreting – consider the information communicated to you.

They say, 'I think it would be best if Sally goes shopping with you as I have a headache.'

There are several ways you might interpret this comment. For example, the speaker has a headache, the speaker does not want to spend time with Sally, or the speaker does not want to go shopping.

If people feel good about themselves because you are responding to them positively, they will be encouraged to tell you more. The more information you gather about someone, the better you will be able to support them.

think about

- What listening skills do you have?
- What listening skills do you need to develop?

did you know?

It is important to respect silences! When you are having a conversation with someone, natural silences give people time to consider the information, reflect on what they have heard and think about their response.

Using visual skills and non-verbal skills

Having good visual skills means that we can observe and notice what is happening around us. Using non-verbal skills means communicating without words – for example, by responding to someone's facial expressions. If you are talking to someone and they screw up their face and frown in response, this might mean they do not like what you are telling them. If you give someone bad news and they smile at you, you should consider whether they have heard you properly and understood the information.

Our body language speaks volumes! Slouching might mean we are uninterested. Bouncing up and down might mean we are happy and excited!

Demonstrate you are listening by giving people eye contact when they are talking to you. If you are looking around the room, the speaker may think that you are uninterested and bored, which will discourage them from continuing.

Make use of gestures when you are listening. For example, nod your head in agreement or put your hand to your mouth in surprise. Gestures show the speaker that they have your attention and that you are fully involved in the conversation.

Using proximity

Proximity means closeness. It is important to be aware of personal space, both yours and that of the person you are communicating with. Being close to someone can be comforting; being too close can be suffocating or threatening and will discourage the person from communicating with you.

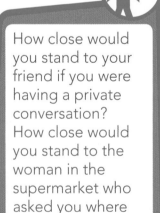

think about

How close would you stand to your friend if you were having a private conversation? How close would you stand to the woman in the supermarket who asked you where the bread was?

Yours.
Mine.

Personal space is important to people

Using touch

Touch is the most frequently used form of non-verbal communication. If we know and trust someone, we are usually comfortable with them being close to us and touching us, so long as it is appropriate.

The people you support will have different ideas about appropriate personal space and touch.

What would you do?

What appropriate physical contact would you use to:
- help somebody with mobility support needs to move from their easy chair to the dining table? (You could put your hand on their back or arm to guide them.)
- support someone who could be at risk of running into a busy road when you are out in the community? (You could link arms with them.)
- support someone to eat who is unable to grip their fork? (You could hold the fork in their hand and guide the hand to their mouth.)
- support someone to change a soiled continence pad? (You could use wipes to clean their bottom.)

Physical contact is not always appropriate and can cause distress. You need to be observant and alert to each individual's response to physical contact. You need to be aware of their personal history. People often have good reasons why physical contact needs to be managed in a particular way.

Ask people if they mind you touching or holding them, and explain how you are going to do this. Check that you have understood each other, and show respect for their privacy and their wishes.

think about

Think of some examples of how we use touch to communicate. For example, shaking hands to say 'welcome', hugging someone to say 'goodbye', or patting someone on the back to say 'well done!'

Tip

REED SOCIAL CARE

In interviews, a firm handshake with good eye contact can be important to a prospective employer – remember: opinions are often formed within the first 10 seconds of meeting somebody!

In Practice

Penny

Penny pops in to see her neighbour, Ray. He is sitting in the front room, the TV is on very loud and all the lights are off.

As Penny walks into the room she says hello to Ray but he seems to ignore her. She moves round so that he can see her and says hello again. He looks up but takes some time to say hello back. Penny turns off the TV, switches on a lamp and pulls a stool nearer to Ray's chair so that she can speak to him.

Penny leans forward on the stool and gently places her hand on Ray's arm; she is very concerned about Ray. She asks him, using a calm but concerned voice, if he is feeling OK.

Which different communication skills does Penny use?

Non-verbal: Penny observes the environment; she notices that the lights are off. This could communicate to her that Ray is confused or unhappy. She changes the environment by switching on the light and turning off the TV so that Ray can concentrate on the conversation.

Verbal: Penny talks to Ray. She uses a calm and concerned voice.

Physical gesture: When she sits next to Ray, Penny puts her hand gently on his arm.

Using reading and writing skills

You will need reading and writing skills to read personal files and communication books, and to write records and support plans.

If you need support with reading and writing, talk to your manager or look at Unit 3 and consider ways to develop your skills in these areas.

4.2 Know how adult social care workers can meet the communication and language needs of individuals

What are the barriers to effective communication and how can you remove these?

Language barriers

Some people use English as an additional language. They may not be able to fully express themselves using English, and their families may not be comfortable speaking in English.

think about

Imagine you are on holiday. When you arrive at your hotel the receptionist cannot find your booking, she does not speak English and you do not speak her language. You do not know the area and your friends are not due to arrive until the next day.
You are stranded, tired and hungry! How does this make you feel?
Frustrated? Angry? Scared?

Imagine you have lost your hearing, and you are unable to speak. How will you communicate the following?

- I am cold.
- I feel unwell.
- I want to watch the television.
- I want to try a new lipstick because I am bored with my old one.

Using a human aid, such as a translator or an advocate, is an effective way to overcome this barrier. A translator translates from one language into another. An advocate supports someone to 'speak up', particularly if they have difficulties communicating. Advocates use a number of different communication tools, including symbols and pictures to help someone ensure that their views and opinions are heard and taken notice of.

Sensory impairment

We use all our senses (seeing, hearing, feeling, smelling and tasting) to communicate. The loss or part loss of any sense creates a communication barrier. For example, hearing loss means that someone may not be able to hear you if you speak to them.

Interpreters can translate spoken words into British Sign Language for people who have a hearing loss.

Technological aids can also support people with sensory loss, such as hearing devices for people with hearing loss, Braille for people with sight loss. Specialist computer software can help people overcome various barriers to communication. Some people use pictures, symbols and sound boards to communicate.

Makaton is a simple form of sign language that was developed for use with people who have learning disabilities and/or limited communication skills.

Use the internet to research communication aids. Try these websites:
www.findavoice.org.uk
www.scope.org.uk/education
www.inclusive.co.uk

Your questions answered

How can I support someone to communicate if they have sight and hearing loss?

Answer: Think about different multi-sensory activities that you could support the person with to encourage communication. For example, creating a herb garden where they can touch and feel the plants, or baking so they can experience the smell and textures of food, and of course the taste! Through these activities they will be able to communicate preferences, likes and dislikes.

Cultural differences

Some people may have communication barriers related to their gender, beliefs or first language. For example, some people find it difficult to talk about their personal care needs with people of the opposite sex.

Some religions say that a woman should only be touched by her close relatives.

It is important that you find out as much as you can about a person's culture and background, as well as their communication preferences, to understand what is appropriate for them. Talk to them, and talk to the people they know well to gather this information.

Hand gestures are a common method of non-verbal communication. However, you must be careful! Some gestures, which may be commonly used in the UK, can be offensive to people from other countries and cultures.
For example: The 'OK' gesture that deep sea divers use, where they touch their index figure and thumb together to indicate that all is well, may seem fairly harmless, but if you are from Brazil or Germany you would be highly offended by this 'obscene' gesture!

How do you think this young man is feeling?

Behaviour and health issues

If people are unhappy or unwell, they may act in a certain way. This may be the effect of their symptoms or because they are unable to express in any other ways that they need support. Be aware of any changes and keep yourself informed by reading communication books and talking to colleagues.

In Practice

Maggie

Since Maggie's mother passed away, the support team at Brook Dean has noticed a number of changes in Maggie's behaviour.

She has started to pick at her arm and has several open sores. She does not sleep well and refuses to eat.

Rachel looks at the staff communication book and notices that this pattern of behaviour has been recorded by several staff over the last few days.

What non-verbal communication is Maggie using?

Answer: Maggie is communicating that she is distressed, and demonstrating this by her choice of behaviour: picking her arm, not sleeping and refusing to eat.

Environmental barriers

Our environment has a significant impact on how we communicate. For example, noisy places can make it difficult for people to hear and be heard; in poor light it is difficult for people to read, or see signs.

Choosing where we communicate is important. It is not appropriate to have a private conversation with someone about their personal care support in a busy café! Not only will there be a risk that strangers will be able to overhear the private conversation, but the supported person could feel uncomfortable and humiliated.

Busy cafés should be avoided when discussing personal care support

think about

Which is the most appropriate place (environment) for each topic of conversation? Choose from: a busy café, doctor's surgery, bus, your kitchen table, pub, office. Some topics will suit more than one location.

- The date you went on last night.
- What outfit to wear to the party tonight.
- The relationship between two of the people you support.
- The score from this afternoon's football match.
- The meal you are going to cook this evening.
- Results of your vaginal smear test / testicular check-up.

4.3 Know the importance of record keeping in adult social care settings

What is the purpose of record keeping? What information do I need to know?

Records are kept to make sure people are supported safely and consistently, in the way they have said they would like to be supported.

Type of record	Knowledge needed to complete the record	Purpose of the record
Medication	Name of individual Type of medication Dosage Day and time administered	To ensure the correct person receives the correct medication in the correct amounts. You will only complete these if you have received training.
Incident and accident books	Names of those involved Date and time of the incident or accident Location Witnesses	To record incidents and accidents To make sure it does not happen again To meet health and safety requirements In case required for legal reasons (insurance or courts)

Type of record	Knowledge needed to complete the record	Purpose of the record

Personal file	Personal and confidential information about an individual including:
	    contact and emergency details
	    health and medication
	    doctors and dentists
	    insurances and end-of-life plans
	    funding and welfare benefits information.
		To maintain information about the individual being supported

Care and support plans	Type, level and frequency of support Support preferences Personal and confidential information Risk assessments	So support staff know how the person wishes to be supported and what care needs this meets

Person-centred plan	Information about the individual's:
	    social networks
	    hopes and dreams
	    fears
	    likes and dislikes.
	Communication and health plans
	Supported decision-making plans
	The support organisation's policies and procedures
		To ensure the supported individual maintains choice and control in their lives

Staff file	Contact information and personal medical / emergency information Qualifications	To record staff information
Petty cash record	Basic numeracy skills A record of money coming in and going out	To manage resources within a given budget. You will only complete this type of record after receiving training.
Staff communication book	Information that needs to be communicated at 'handover' between shifts	To ensure that information and messages are recorded and accessed by all staff
Individual communication diary	Information about supported individuals and any issues or information that support workers need to be aware of	To ensure consistent support between support workers
Visitors' attendance book	Name and date of people entering and leaving the building	To meet fire regulations

Some of the records that adult social care workers need to keep

did you know?

Care plans are legal documents that may be required in court. They act as signed contracts between the individual who is being supported and the organisation that agrees to meet the assessed eligible needs of that individual.

In Practice

Josh

Josh leaves a message for Rachel in the daily staff communication book. When Rachel comes in she tries to read it but Josh's handwriting is very messy.

Rachel reads the message as best as she can: 'Can you ___ another & boxes of ___ please I ____ordered __.'

Rachel is really confused. What is Josh asking her to do? What has Josh ordered?

The message should read: 'Can you order another 8 boxes of gloves please, I haven't ordered any.'

Tip

REED
SOCIAL CARE

Now is an ideal time to begin to think about constructing your CV. The information you provide should be relevant, clear and concise. (Don't forget to take notice of the advice offered in the Tip boxes throughout this book.) For more information on constructing a CV, visit www.reed.co.uk

What record keeping skills do you need?

Making sure that records are accurate

Inaccurate information could be harmful for the people you support. Records should be accurate and:

- understandable – poor handwriting causes mistakes

- relevant – only give information that is asked for

- clear and concise

- factual – do not include your personal opinions. Never make up or exaggerate anything

- free of errors – check personal information is up to date, and that all information is accurate

- signed and dated – only sign something you have completed yourself, and don't change anything unless you have permission.

In Practice

Anna

Anna has been diagnosed with an allergy to dairy products. She can no longer eat cheese, butter, yogurt or cow's milk.

Anna's support worker, Rachel, immediately updates all Anna's personal files, menu plans, shopping lists and emergency information. She then writes in the staff communication book, alerting all staff to read Anna's personal file immediately before they begin their shift.

Fariah starts work that morning, a little later than normal as she had a dental appointment first thing. When she arrives at work all the other staff are supporting people to wash in the bathrooms. Anna is sitting at the kitchen table on her own.

Anna does not use verbal communication but lifts her hand to her mouth, telling Fariah that she would like a drink. Fariah pours Anna a glass of milk.

She is about to support Anna to drink the milk when Rachel comes into the kitchen and immediately tells Fariah to stop. Luckily Anna has not yet drunk any of the milk. If she had done, she would have been very poorly.

Fariah should have read the staff communication book before she started her shift.

Understandable
Relevant to purpose
Clear and concise
Factual
Checkable

Recording information correctly

Making sure that information is kept confidential and secure

Organisations in social care have a legal responsibility to keep certain information they hold about people confidential and secure. See Unit 2 for more information about confidentiality.

A UK residential care home group

All our staff need to be able to write concise, professional, accurate records of everything they do: it's absolutely essential. We keep records of everything from medication given to food preferences. Good records can mean the difference between life and death, as well as providing the right level of respect to our users, so we would expect every member of staff to take the time to write accurate reports. You can often tell the ability of somebody to write good reports from the quality of their CV; I look for a CV to be concise, well written and informative, without going into too much detail or providing irrelevant information.

@work

Quick Quiz

1 What is a communication passport?
 a. A booklet that gives someone permission to speak at meetings
 b. A personal communication diary
 c. A record of how someone chooses to communicate
 d. A photograph album

2 Which of the following is NOT a communication skill?
 a. Talking
 b. Riding a bike
 c. Using sign language
 d. Listening

3 What is NOT a part of active listening?
 a. Eye contact
 b. Interrupting people
 c. Repeating things back
 d. Interpreting information

4 Which of the following is NOT a non-verbal communication tool?
 a. Speaking
 b. Gesturing
 c. Smiling
 d. Body language

5 When is it NOT appropriate for social care workers to use touch to communicate?
 a. To comfort someone when they are upset
 b. To hold them down when they are angry
 c. To gently attract someone's attention
 d. To guide someone away from danger

6 Which of the following is NOT one of our five senses?
 a. Seeing
 c. Laughing
 b. Hearing
 d. Tasting

7 Which of these is NOT a barrier to communication?
 a. Sensory loss
 b. Having English as an additional language
 c. Feeling unwell
 d. A mobile phone

8 What should we NOT do when we complete records within adult social care?
 a. Be accurate
 b. Write clearly
 c. Use only factual information
 d. Write information about our personal opinions

9 What kinds of record are NOT kept in social care?
 a. Medical records
 b. Support and care plans
 c. Notes about food preferences
 d. Daily communication books

10 What is the Data Protection Act?
 a. A law that prevents us from collecting personal information
 b. A law that protects people's personal information
 c. A law that requires us to send information to the government
 d. A law that requires people to keep personal information in a locked safe

Unit 5

Awareness of the
role and responsibilities
of the
adult social care worker

The aim of this unit is to develop your awareness and understanding of the roles and responsibilities of adult social care workers.

You will look at the role of social care workers and how they support individuals from day to day.

Partnership working is investigated, together with the benefits of this for the individual and others involved in their support. You will also learn why it is important to report any concerns you have about an individual's safety.

On completion of this unit you will:

- know about the responsibilities of the adult social care worker
- know about the role of the adult social care worker.

5.1 Know about the responsibilities of the adult social care worker

Social care workers must work in line with the General Social Care Council's (GSCC) code of practice.

The GSCC code of practice requires that social care workers must:

1. Protect the rights and promote the interests of individuals and carers

2. Strive to establish and maintain the trust and confidence of individuals and carers

3. Promote the independence of individuals while protecting them as far as possible from danger or harm

4. Respect the rights of individuals while seeking to ensure that their behaviour does not harm themselves or other people

5. Uphold public trust and confidence in social care services

6. Be accountable for the quality of their work and take responsibility for maintaining and improving their knowledge and skills.

Tip

REED
SOCIAL CARE

At this stage, you should consider where you may have undertaken responsibilities elsewhere in your life, for example, meeting deadlines in your course studies, or working as part of a team in sports or social events.

How is your working relationship with the people you support different from the relationships you have with your close friends?

Two major differences between relationships with the people you support and friendships in your private life are:

- you are paid a salary to work, and sign a contract to say you will carry out your duties as a social care worker in line with the code of conduct
- you must never accept gifts or money from the people you support.

As an adult social care worker your responsibilities will include a wide range of duties and tasks that you must undertake in a timely manner, and within legal and organisational guidelines. Remember, it is your responsibility to seek support whenever you are unsure or need more information about your duties at work.

How can you support professional relationships?

It is important that you always work within professional boundaries.

If you build special relationships with people, this may be viewed as favouritism, and this isn't supporting people fairly and equally. You are in a position of trust and you must always be aware of the 'power' you could hold over individuals. Your professional relationship with the people you support is very different from the relationships you have with your family and friends.

You will need to know when you should 'step away' and you must be clear on the dangers of over-involvement. Supporting someone to maintain their independence cannot happen if they become dependent on you. It's great to build relationships with people, but it's harmful when people won't eat or wash unless you are on shift! What would happen if you left to take a different job somewhere else?

This doesn't mean that you can't genuinely care for or have concern for someone you support. This is a valuable attitude to have when working in social care. You just need to be aware of how to balance and separate your private and professional lives. You need to be clear on your responsibility to support the people you work with to live their own lives and to develop their own relationships.

You will also need to know when to maintain the confidentiality of the people you support and when to breach it. There is more on this in Unit 2.

Partnerships

Partnership working is essential for sharing information and providing support as part of a team. It is important that everyone works in partnership to ensure that the person being supported is at the centre of all discussions and planning about them.

You should respect the skills of other team members – all the people you work with will have a valued role to play in supporting people to achieve and maintain a good quality of life.

> **Partnership working** Working alongside other people – for example, the people you support; their family and close friends; your colleagues; other professionals, agencies and organisations providing home services, such as meals on wheels.
>
> **Key Term**

Tip

REED SOCIAL CARE

In an interview, you may want to describe experiences you have had when volunteering in another organisation. Be careful not to disclose any confidential information about the organisation or its individuals. Examples should be given without names or specifics – the same goes for your CV.

Tip

REED SOCIAL CARE

Creating a strong CV centred on roles and responsibilities that you have undertaken is essential when applying for a position in adult social care. Find out about and volunteer for work in your local area which you can use to increase your understanding of the roles you wish to undertake.

Imagine you have to write a plan for your life for the next year.

- Who would you want to help you plan?

- What if you have to make an important decision about your health? Who would you want to help you to do that?

- How would you feel if decisions about your life were made without you?

As a member of the team, make sure you support members of the staff team, communicate appropriately and record information accurately. You may need to help the people you support to manage and resolve any issues they have with external agencies.

In Practice

Ray

Ray has not been very well recently. His neighbour, Penny, has been concerned about him. She contacts social services and speaks to a social worker in the Older People's Social Work team.

Rob, the social worker, contacts Ray and suggests that a few people get together to talk about what life is like for Ray now, what is going well for him, and what needs to change. He asks Ray who he would like to come to the meeting.

Ray says he would like Penny, his neighbour, and his daughter to be at the meeting. Rob suggests Ray might like to ask the community nurse and the occupational therapist to come too.

This mixture of professionals, family and friends – and, of course, Ray – will work in partnership to help Ray think about his life now and how he would like to be supported.

Examples of 'multi-partnership' are:
- multi-agency: different agencies working together
- multi-disciplinary: teams of different professionals working together.

Reporting abuse

Abuse is a wide term and takes many different forms. It can be when someone is physically hurt, or when the abuse affects a person's mental well-being. It can be something that happens frequently or as a one-off occurrence. The seven areas (or categories) of abuse are shown in the table below.

You don't have to be 100 per cent sure that abuse is taking place; you should voice your concerns to your manager even if you only suspect abuse is taking place.

Category of abuse	What might have happened	Indicators (signs)
1 Physical	Physical violence Medical mistreatment	Unexplained bruises, marks, burns, changes in behaviour, changes in routine
2 Neglect	Failure to provide adequate food and water or personal care	Weight loss, complaints of pain, anxiety, depression, changes in sleeping routine
3 Sexual	Rape, sexual assault, exposure, offensive language	Genital pain, discharge or bleeding, bruising in intimate areas
4 Financial and material	Stealing money or possessions, denying access to money	Money and possessions missing, secrecy over access to records
5 Psychological or emotional	Threats, bullying, being 'made fun of', lying	Low self-esteem, lack of confidence, self-harm, lack of trust in others
6 Discrimination	Offensive name-calling, not meeting dietary needs, not allowing attendance at religious services or festivals	Rejection of food and activities that are not appropriate, low self-esteem, lack of self-confidence
7 Institutional	Lack of flexibility, rigid routines, failure to meet basic needs, confinement	Afraid to make complaints Loss of skills, withdrawal, loss of communication skills

The seven categories of abuse with common indicators, or signs, to alert you that someone may be being abused

All abuse must be taken seriously – even minor acts can have a devastating and long-term effect on the person who has been abused. Abuse can happen at any time and in any place – and the people who abuse do not do it openly.

Discovering or being told that someone is being abused will not be a very pleasant experience. You may be shocked, frightened, angry or confused. You may even question whether or not you are being told the truth.

But you must act quickly to support the individual concerned; you are responsible for their safety.

You must tell someone else.

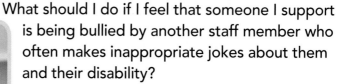

Your questions answered

What should I do if I feel that someone I support is being bullied by another staff member who often makes inappropriate jokes about them and their disability?

Answer: You should talk to your supervisor or manager and raise your concerns.

5.2 Know about the role of the adult social care worker

Daily tasks

Depending on your job, there will be a range of tasks and activities that you will need to undertake.

These include:

- helping with personal care
- supporting individuals to maintain their personal hygiene
- serving meals and supporting people to eat
- doing household chores, such as cleaning and laundry
- setting up activities to support individuals
- supporting people with various activities
- working alongside family, friends and other professionals within the setting
- visiting professionals
- completing and maintaining accurate and timely records.

Tip

REED
SOCIAL CARE

When applying for a position in an organisation, ensure that you ask questions about the precise nature of the role before the interview. This will give you time to think of examples of where you have undertaken relevant activities in the past.

find out!

Look again at the 'In Practice' sections on pages 23, 25 and 42 for more examples of the daily tasks adult social care workers undertake.

Part of the duty of care is to give appropriate support at the right time

Your duty of care

Adult social care workers have a duty of care to provide support safely, appropriately and in a timely manner. To ensure you meet these responsibilities, you will need to:

● develop a good understanding of the policies and procedures within your organisation that you are expected to uphold

● monitor and review anything that may impact on your duty of care

● be aware of the health and safety of the people you support. You will also be expected to take reasonable care of your own safety

- ensure you receive training on health and safety. This is required, by law

- only take on work and tasks that you are trained to do, and seek help for those that you are not trained or able to perform

- keep accurate records and report accidents, incidents and concerns

- always act in the best interest of the individuals you support

- don't wait before it's too late to take action.

Failing to look after someone for whom you have a duty of care is 'neglect'. This could be failing to notice that someone has a sore on their foot which becomes seriously infected, or not supporting someone to keep clean for weeks.

find out!

Use the internet to find out more about the adult social worker's duty of care.

did you know?

Health and Safety legislation (laws) includes rules about:
- how to safely move and handle people and equipment
- how to store and use hazardous substances, for example cleaning fluids
- first aid
- food safety
- fire safety.

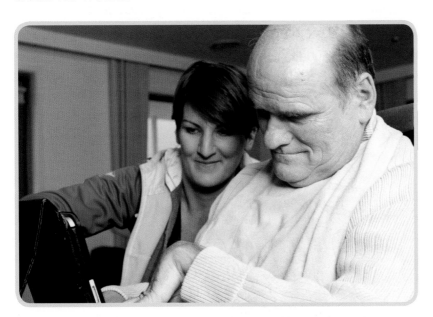

Be aware of individuals that may need your support

Person-centred support

The key to meeting your roles and responsibilities as an adult social care worker is to make sure that you offer person-centred support. You need to support people to make choices about how they live their lives. It is not possible to know how someone wishes to be supported unless you ask them and the people who know them well.

think about

How would you ensure the people you support are treated in a person-centred way?
Start by looking at the situation from the individual's point of view. We don't all want the same things!

You will need to involve people you support in decision making. Find out how they choose to communicate and then find out about their hopes for life, what they like or dislike. To do this you will need to spend time with them and use different person-centred approaches.

Person-centred planning helps people to make decisions and stay in control of their lives

The guiding principles of person-centred support are:

- choice and control – ensure that the person is at the centre of all decision making. For example, an individual may choose not to be part of an activity. You will need to respect an individual's wishes, likes and dislikes around the timing of daily activities

- setting goals

- learning – consider ways in which you can support someone to try new things and learn new skills

- listening – find out what people want and what their aspirations are

- information – supporting people in a person-centred way is a great opportunity to gather information about a person; for example, who they are, their history, their hopes and fears

- being positive – think about what people *can* do and what they are good at. Find out how other people describe the person's good points. Think about any risks in a positive way; consider how they can be managed so that the risk reduces

- good relationships – support people to develop and maintain relationships

- flexibility – person-centred support is not about 'fitting' people into existing services! It is about finding out how somebody wants to be supported, where they want to spend time, and who they want to support them so that they can lead the kind of life that they choose.

find out!

Find out more about person-centred support and planning on the website www. in-control.org.uk

Describe your idea of 'a good day'.

- Where are you?
- What are you doing?
- Who are you with?
- How do you feel?

Now think about Liz. Liz is having 'a bad day'. She is tired because her mattress is uncomfortable but no one has noticed; she is hungry because she didn't want soup for lunch and people assumed that she just didn't want lunch. She is in a supermarket surrounded by noise and bright lights, which Liz finds distressing. Also, she is cold because the support staff forgot to bring her coat.

- How do you think Liz is feeling?

If you started a new job tomorrow, and your job was to support Liz:

- How would you make sure that tomorrow is 'a good day' for Liz?

Coventry City Council

Person-centred care

Coventry City Council's person-centred support places the people who use our services at the centre of all decisions, ensuring their care package is holistic and meets the needs of the individual, not the service itself. In Coventry, customer focus is essential in all we do, which is why our packages of support are so individualised. Our staff need to understand that.

@work

Quick Quiz

1   Which of the following is NOT considered the responsibility of a social care worker?
    a. Protecting the rights of people they support
    b. Establishing and maintaining people's confidence
    c. Accepting gifts from people that receive support
    d. Being accountable for their work

2   How is an adult social care worker's professional relationship with the people they support different from the relationships they have with their family and friends? Choose ONE.
    a. They are not allowed to like the people they support
    b. They wouldn't choose to be friends with the people they support
    c. They like to be seen as superior to the people they support
    d. A person's family and friends do not expect them to be professional and accountable at all times

3   Who would you NOT work with if you were working 'in partnership' within adult social care?
    a. Your colleagues
    b. The people you support and their families
    c. Health professionals
    d. No one

4   Which of the following is NOT a category of abuse?
    a. Discrimination
    b. Institutionalisation
    c. Neglect
    d. Exercise

5   Which of the following tasks is NOT part of the role of an adult social care worker?
    a. Support someone to change their continence pad
    b. Diagnose mental health problems
    c. Cook a roast dinner for eight people
    d. Support someone to eat by liquidising their food

6   What is NOT part of an adult social worker's duty of care?
    a. Health and safety checks
    b. Completing tasks that you are not yet qualified to do
    c. Maintaining accurate records
    d. Keeping your professional learning and development up to date

7   Which of the following is NOT an activity to ensure health and safety in the workplace?
    a. Checking equipment is safe to use
    b. Wearing gloves when supporting people with their personal care
    c. Cooking enough roast potatoes for eight people
    d. Knowing where the fire exits are and the evacuation procedure in case of fire

8   Person-centred support is NOT about which of the following?
    a. What the individual likes and dislikes
    b. The supported person's aspirations
    c. What time the individual needs to go to bed to fit in with staff shift patterns
    d. How a person chooses to communicate

9   Person-centred support is NOT about which of the following?
    a. Setting goals
    b. Offering positive support
    c. Doing things 'to' rather than 'with' people
    d. Flexible support to meet needs

10 What should you do if you think you may not be clear on your responsibilities as a social care worker? Choose TWO.
    a. Panic
    b. Lose confidence
    c. Think about specific areas that you may need extra training and support in
    d. Ask your manager for advice

Ready for work?

Throughout this course you have been furnished with the tools to successfully apply for positions within the adult social care sector.

What follows is a checklist of things you should have done during the course to ensure that you are well placed to successfully apply and interview for the positions which interest you.

Checklist

☑ **CV** – produce a concise, well presented CV that complies with data confidentiality (see reed.co.uk for advice).

☑ **Work experience** – try to obtain some voluntary work experience to strengthen your application. Speak to local organisations to see if you can work with them.

☑ **Research** – make a list of local companies that you feel you would like to work for and find out what they do. Researching these companies at this stage will make applying to work for them later much easier. It will also help a recruitment agency find a suitable position for you if you have a good understanding of the types of organisation you would like to work for.

☑ **Extra activities** – think about extra activities that you have done or could do to strengthen your CV by demonstrating leadership skills, inspiration and improvement.

☑ **Weaknesses** – think about any areas in your skills and experience that you feel could be improved. These are essential for interview, and you should also think about ways to improve them.

☑ **Interview practice** – practise interview questions with your friends or family, to improve your confidence when you attend the real thing. Look online at reed.co.uk for tips on interview questions, and example questions that you might be asked.

☑ **Personal Development Plan (PDP)** – create a PDP, detailing your training experience and courses that you would like to take in the future. This will help you to have a clear idea about where you would like your career to go. This kind of information can also be helpful to any recruitment agency that you may choose to visit.

☑ **References** – these are essential if you want to work in the social care sector. As you come to the end of any voluntary work, make sure you obtain the details of somebody you can ask for a reference when applying for future jobs. Also, keep track of people from your time in education – if you do not have much professional experience, educational references will be important. You should keep a list of these references in your work pack – they will be asked for by both recruitment agencies and any prospective employers that you apply to work for.

Applying for jobs

Now that you have successfully created your CV using advice from reed.co.uk, you are ready to start applying for jobs. The following checklist gives a number of steps that you should take to ensure that you have the best chance of finding the job you want.

Checklist

☑ **Set up email alerts** – use reed.co.uk to set up an email alert which will come through to you when new jobs are posted in the social care sector. This will enable you to apply quickly when new jobs are posted, as well as keeping you aware of opportunities in the market.

☑ **Apply for jobs online** – using reed.co.uk, search for positions in the social care sector that are near where you live. If you find something that interests you, then apply! Write a brief covering letter to accompany your CV – make sure that it makes specific reference to the position that you are applying for, but don't make it too long.

☑ **Register with your local Reed Social Care branch** – phone or visit them to make an appointment to do this. When meeting a consultant, ensure that you take along all the documentation that you have been asked to bring – you won't be able to register without it. Registering with a Reed consultant means that you increase your chances of finding the right job for you. You should be honest about your skills and experience, as that will aid the consultant in matching you to jobs that would interest and benefit you. Reed Social Care has a variety of temporary and permanent positions available throughout the UK.

Glossary

Abbreviation A shortened word, such as 'meds' for medication.

Belief A principle that an individual holds and believes to be true.

Body language The position and movements of someone's body when they are communicating. People are generally unaware of their body language and it often reveals how they are really feeling.

Care plan A document outlining how a person is to be supported.

Care worker Someone who is employed and trained to provide care and support.

Carer Someone who provides informal care.

Communication passport A record of how an individual chooses to communicate. They may use words, gestures, pictures or behaviour.

Community hub A centre managed by three or more groups which work to improve the quality of life for the whole community. Similar to a drop-in centre.

Discrimination When individuals are treated differently, unfairly or unequally because of their disability, age, gender, race or sexuality.

Duty of care Health and social care organisations have a duty of care towards the people they support. They must ensure that they are safe from harm. Adult social care workers have a duty of care to provide support safely, appropriately and in a timely manner.

Empower Enable someone to take control and make decisions about their life.

Enable Support someone by providing them with the means, knowledge and opportunity to continue to do as much as possible for themselves for as long as they can.

Holistic approach Considering a person's whole life, not just parts of it.

Inequality Unfair differences (not equal) where one group or individual has less of something than another group or individual.

Jargon Words used in a particular profession that may not mean anything to someone outside that profession.

Multicultural Including people of different races, languages and religions.

Outcome The result achieved from an action.

Partnership Working together with another person or an organisation.

Partnership working Working alongside other people – for example, the supported individual and their family and close friends; colleagues; other professionals, agencies and organisations providing home services.

Personal budget An amount of money provided by the local authority and given directly to an individual so they can arrange their own support.

Personal history Information about a person and their background – their wishes for the future, their likes, dislikes, dreams and fears.

Person-centred When someone is involved in any discussion about their life, with their needs and wishes placed at the centre of that discussion.

Prejudice An opinion that is held without knowing or considering all the information available.

Principle A guiding rule or belief for personal behaviour, often based on a person's culture and religion. Principles shape what people believe to be right or wrong.

Quality of life A good quality of life is having a good standard of health and well-being, with opportunities to access education, work and leisure.

Respite A short period of time when an individual or their carer can have a break.

Review When an individual and their support circle consider the support they have been receiving and whether or not it meets their support needs.

Skill The ability to do something and to do it well.

Slang The use of informal words, such as 'grub' instead of 'food'.

Stereotype A fixed idea about a type of person.

Support plan See *Care plan.*

Supported decision making When an individual is given support to make decisions; for example, deciding what to wear or eat, or where to live.

Value A standard of behaviour that an individual believes to be important. Values influence everything people do.

Vulnerable adult A person over the age of 18 'who is or may be in need of community care services by reason of mental or other disability, age or illness; and who is or may be unable to take care of him or herself, or unable to protect him or herself against significant harm or exploitation'.

Index